W9-BJV-517

The Selected Poems

1951–1977

A. R. AMMONS

The Selected Poems

1951–1977

W · W · NORTON & COMPANY · INC ·

NEW YORK

Published simultaneously in Canada by George J. McLeod Limited, To-
ronto. Printed in the United States of America.

Library of Congress Cataloging in Publication Data

Ammons, A   R   1926–
   The selected poems, 1951–1977.

PS3501.M6A6 1977   811'.5'4   77–22456
ISBN 0–393–04465–3
ISBN 0–393–04470–X pbk.

3 4 5 6 7 8 9 0

to Frederick Morgan

Contents

The Selected Poems

1951–1977

So I Said I Am Ezra

So I said I am Ezra
and the wind whipped my throat
gaming for the sounds of my voice
   I listened to the wind
go over my head and up into the night
Turning to the sea I said
       I am Ezra
but there were no echoes from the waves
The words were swallowed up
  in the voice of the surf
or leaping over the swells
lost themselves oceanward
   Over the bleached and broken fields
I moved my feet and turning from the wind
   that ripped sheets of sand
   from the beach and threw them
   like seamists across the dunes
swayed as if the wind were taking me away
and said
       I am Ezra
As a word too much repeated
falls out of being
so I Ezra went out into the night
like a drift of sand
and splashed among the windy oats
that clutch the dunes
of unremembered seas

Bees Stopped

Bees stopped on the rock
and rubbed their headparts and wings
rested then flew on:
ants ran over the whitish greenish reddish
plants that grow flat on rocks
and people never see
because nothing should grow on rocks:
I looked out over the lake
and beyond to the hills and trees
and nothing was moving
so I looked closely
along the lakeside
under the old leaves of rushes
and around clumps of drygrass
and life was everywhere
so I went on sometimes whistling

The Pieces of My Voice

The pieces of my voice have been thrown
away I said turning to the hedgerows
and hidden ditches
Where do the pieces of
my voice lie scattered
The cedarcone said you have been ground
down into and whirled

Tomorrow I must go look under the clumps of
marshgrass in wet deserts
and in dry deserts
when the wind falls from the mountain
inquire of the chuckwalla what he saw go by
and what the sidewinder found
risen in the changing sand
I must run down all the pieces
and build the whole silence back

As I look across the fields the sun
big in my eyes I see the hills
the great black unwasting silence and
know I must go out beyond the hills and seek
for I am broken over the earth—
so little remains
for the silent offering of my death

Coming to Sumer

Coming to Sumer and the tamarisks on the river
I Ezra with unsettling love
rifled the mud and wattle huts
for recent mournings
with gold leaves
and lapis lazuli beads
in the neat braids loosening from the skull
    Looking through the wattles to the sun
I said
It has rained some here in this place
unless snow falls heavily in the hills
to do this
    The floor was smooth with silt
and river weeds hanging gray
on the bent reeds spoke saying
Everything is even here as you can see
    Firing the huts
I abandoned the unprofitable poor
unequal even in the bone
    to disrespect
    and casual with certainty
watched an eagle wing as I went
to king and priest

In the Wind My Rescue Is

In the wind my rescue is
in whorls of it
    like winged tufts of dreams
bearing
   through the forms of nothingness
   the gyres and hurricane eyes
the seed safety
    of multiple origins

I set it my task
to gather the stones of earth
    into one place
the water modeled sand molded stones
   from
     the water images
     of riverbeds in drought
   from the boundaries of the mind
   from
     sloping farms
     and altitudes of ice and
to mount upon the highest stone
a cardinal
chilled in the attitude of song

But the wind has sown loose dreams
in my eyes
    and telling unknown tongues
drawn me out beyond the land's end
    and rising in long
   parabolas of bliss
borne me safety
from all those ungathered stones

I Came Upon a Plateau

I came upon a plateau
where mesquite roots
crazed the stone
   and rains
moved glinting dust
down the crevices
   Calling off rings
      to a council of peaks
I said
Spare me man's redundancy
and putting on bright clothes
sat down in the flat orthodoxy

Quivering with courtesy
a snake drew thrust in sines
and circles from his length
rearing coils of warning white
   Succumbing in the still ecstasy
sinuous through white rows of scales
I caved in upon eternity
saying this use is colorless

A pious person his heart
looted and burnt
     sat under a foundation
a windy cloak clutched round his bones
and said
When the razed temple cooled
I went in
and gathered these
relics of holy urns

Behold beneath this cloak
  and I looked in
at the dark whirls of dust

The peaks coughing bouldered
laughter shook to pieces
and the snake shed himself in ripples
across a lake of sand

Choice

Idling through the mean space dozing,
blurred by indirection, I came upon a
stairwell and steadied a moment to
think against the stem:
upward turned golden steps
and downward dark steps entered the dark:

unused to other than even ground I
spurned the airless heights though bright
and the rigor to lift an immaterial soul
and sank
sliding in a smooth rail whirl and fell
asleep in the inundating dark
but waking said god abhors me
but went on down obeying at least
the universal law of gravity:

millenniums later waking in a lightened air
I shivered in high purity
and still descending grappled with
the god that
rolls up circles of our linear
sight in crippling disciplines
tighter than any climb.

Hymn

I know if I find you I will have to leave the earth
and go on out
        over the sea marshes and the brant in bays
and over the hills of tall hickory
and over the crater lakes and canyons
and on up through the spheres of diminishing air
past the blackset noctilucent clouds
                where one wants to stop and look
way past all the light diffusions and bombardments
up farther than the loss of sight
        into the unseasonal undifferentiated empty stark

And I know if I find you I will have to stay with the earth
inspecting with thin tools and ground eyes
trusting the microvilli sporangia and simplest
        coelenterates
and praying for a nerve cell
with all the soul of my chemical reactions
and going right on down where the eye sees only traces

You are everywhere partial and entire
You are on the inside of everything and on the outside

I walk down the path down the hill where the sweetgum
has begun to ooze spring sap at the cut
and I see how the bark cracks and winds like no other bark
chasmal to my ant-soul running up and down
and if I find you I must go out deep into your
        far resolutions
and if I find you I must stay here with the separate leaves

The Wide Land

Having split up the chaparral
blasting my sight
the wind said
   You know I'm
     the result of
forces beyond my control
I don't hold it against you
I said
It's all right I understand

Those pressure bowls and cones
the wind said
are giants in their continental gaits
I know I said I know
they're blind giants
Actually the wind said I'm
   if anything beneficial
     resolving extremes
filling up lows with highs
No I said you don't have
to explain
It's just the way things are

Blind in the wide land I
turned and risked my feet
to loose stones and sudden

alterations of height

Gravelly Run

I don't know somehow it seems sufficient
to see and hear whatever coming and going is,
losing the self to the victory
    of stones and trees,
of bending sandpit lakes, crescent
round groves of dwarf pine:

for it is not so much to know the self
as to know it as it is known
    by galaxy and cedar cone,
as if birth had never found it
and death could never end it:

the swamp's slow water comes
down Gravelly Run fanning the long
    stone-held algal
hair and narrowing roils between
the shoulders of the highway bridge:

holly grows on the banks in the woods there,
and the cedars' gothic-clustered
    spires could make
green religion in winter bones:

so I look and reflect, but the air's glass
jail seals each thing in its entity:

no use to make any philosophies here:
    I see no
god in the holly, hear no song from
the snowbroken weeds: Hegel is not the winter
yellow in the pines: the sunlight has never
heard of trees: surrendered self among
    unwelcoming forms: stranger,
hoist your burdens, get on down the road.

Prospecting

(1) Coming to cottonwoods, an
orange rockshelf,
and in the gully
an edging of stream willows,

(2) I made camp
and turned my mule loose
to graze in the dark
evening of the mountain.

(3) Drowsed over the coals
and my loneliness
like an inner image went
out and shook
hands with the willows,

(4) and running up the black scarp
tugged the heavy moon
up and over into light,

(5) and on a hill-thorn of sage
called with the coyotes
and told ghost stories to
a night circle of lizards.
Tipping on its handle
the Dipper unobtrusively
poured out the night.

(6) At dawn returning, wet
to the hips with meetings,
my loneliness woke me up
and we merged refreshed into
the breaking of camp and day.

The Wind Coming Down From

summit and blue air
said I am sorry for you
and lifting past
    said you
are mere dust which I
    as you see control

yet nevertheless are
    instrument of miracle

and rose
    out of earshot but
returning in a slow loop
    said while
I am always just this bunch of
    compensating laws
pushed, pushing
    not air or motion
but the motion of air

I coughed
    and the wind said
Ezra will live
to see your last
    sun come up again

I turned (as I will) to weeds and
the wind went off
    carving
monuments through a field of stone
    monuments whose shape

wind cannot arrest but
taking hold on
   changes

while Ezra
   listens from terraces of mind
wind cannot reach or
weedroots of my low-feeding shiver

Terminus

Coming to a rockwall
I looked back
to the winding gulch
and said
is this as far as you can go:

and the gulch, rubble
frazzled with the windy remains
of speech, said
comers here turn and go back:

so I sat down, resolved
to try
the problem out, and
every leaf fell
from my bush of bones

and sand blew down the winding
gulch and
eddying
rounded out a bowl
from the terminal wall:

I sat in my bones' fragile shade
and worked the
knuckles of my mind till
the altering earth broke to
mend the fault:

I rose and went through.

Possibility Along a Line of Difference

At the crustal
discontinuity
I went down and
walked
on the gravel bottom,
head below gully rims

tufted with
clumpgrass and
through-free roots:
prairie flatness crazed
by that difference,
I grew

excited with
the stream's image left
in dust
and farther down
in confined rambling
I

found a puddle
green, iridescent
with a visitation of daub-singing wasps,
sat down and watched
tilted shadow untilting
fill the trough,

imagined cloudbursts
and
scattered pillars of rain,
buffalo at night routed
by lightning,
leaping,

falling back,
wobble-kneed calves
tumbling, gully-caught;
coyote, crisp-footed
on the gravel,
loping up the difference.

Mansion

So it came time
        for me to cede myself
and I chose
the wind
        to be delivered to

The wind was glad
        and said it needed all
the body
it could get
        to show its motions with

and wanted to know
        willingly as I hoped it would
if it could do
something in return
        to show its gratitude

When the tree of my bones
        rises from the skin I said
come and whirlwinding
stroll my dust
        around the plain

so I can see
        how the ocotillo does
and how saguaro-wren is
and when you fall
        with evening

fall with me here
        where we can watch
the closing up of day
and think how morning breaks

Prodigal

After the shifts and dis-
continuities, after the congregations of orders,
    black masses floating through
    mind's boreal clarity, icebergs in fog,
flotillas of wintering ducks weathering the night,
    chains of orders, multifilamentous chains
    knobbed with possibility, disoriented
chains, winding back on themselves, unwinding,
    intervolving, spinning, breaking off

    (nomads clustering at dusk into tents of sleep,
disorganizing, widening out again with morning)
    after the mental

    blaze and gleam,
the mind in both motions building and tearing down,
    running to link effective chains,
    establish molecules of meaning,
frameworks, to
    perfect modes of structuring
    (so days can bend to trellising
and pruned take shape,
    bloom into necessary event)

    after these motions, these vectors,
orders moving in and out of orders, collisions
    of orders, dispersions, the grasp weakens,

    the mind whirls, short of the unifying
reach, short of the heat
    to carry that forging:

after the visions of these losses, the spent
seer, delivered to wastage, risen
   into ribs, consigns knowledge to
   approximation, order to the vehicle
of change, and fumbles blind in blunt innocence
   toward divine, terrible love.

Mechanism

Honor a going thing, goldfinch, corporation, tree,
      morality: any working order,
    animate or inanimate: it

has managed directed balance,
      the incoming and outgoing energies are working right,
    some energy left to the mechanism,

some ash, enough energy held
      to maintain the order in repair,
    assure further consumption of entropy,

expending energy to strengthen order:
      honor the persisting reactor,
    the container of change, the moderator: the yellow

bird flashes black wing-bars
      in the new-leaving wild cherry bushes by the bay,
    startles the hawk with beauty,

flitting to a branch where
      flash vanishes into stillness,
    hawk addled by the sudden loss of sight:

honor the chemistries, platelets, hemoglobin kinetics,
      the light-sensitive iris, the enzymic intricacies
    of control,

the gastric transformations, seed
      dissolved to acrid liquors, synthesized into
    chirp, vitreous humor, knowledge,

blood compulsion, instinct: honor the
     unique genes,
   molecules that reproduce themselves, divide into

sets, the nucleic grain transmitted
     in slow change through ages of rising and falling form,
   some cells set aside for the special work, mind

or perception rising into orders of courtship,
     territorial rights, mind rising
   from the physical chemistries

to guarantee that genes will be exchanged, male
     and female met, the satisfactions cloaking a deeper
   racial satisfaction:

heat kept by a feathered skin:
     the living alembic, body heat maintained (bunsen
   burner under the flask)

so the chemistries can proceed, reaction rates
     interdependent, self-adjusting, with optimum
   efficiency—the vessel firm, the flame

staying: isolated, contained reactions! the precise and
     necessary worked out of random, reproducible,
   the handiwork redeemed from chance, while the

goldfinch, unconscious of the billion operations
     that stay its form, flashes, chirping (not a
   great songster) in the bay cherry bushes wild of leaf.

Guide

You cannot come to unity and remain material:
in that perception is no perceiver:
   when you arrive
you have gone too far:
         at the Source you are in the mouth of Death:

you cannot
   turn around in
the Absolute: there are no entrances or exits
         no precipitations of forms
to use like tongs against the formless:
   no freedom to choose:

to be
         you have to stop not-being and break
off from *is* to *flowing* and
   this is the sin you weep and praise:
origin is your original sin:
         the return you long for will ease your guilt
and you will have your longing:

   the wind that is my guide said this: it
should know having
         given up everything to eternal being but
direction:

how I said can I be glad and sad: but a man goes
   from one foot to the other:
wisdom wisdom:
         to be glad and sad at once is also unity
and death:

wisdom wisdom: a peachblossom blooms on a particular
tree on a particular day:
         unity cannot do anything in particular:

are these the thoughts you want me to think I said but
    the wind was gone and there was no more knowledge then.

Terrain

The soul is a region without definite boundaries:
   it is not certain a prairie
can exhaust it
         or a range enclose it:
it floats (self-adjusting) like the continental mass,
   where it towers most
extending its deepest mantling base
         (exactly proportional):
does not flow all one way: there is a divide:
   river systems thrown like winter tree-shadows
against the hills: branches, runs, high lakes:
         stagnant lily-marshes:

is variable, has weather: floods unbalancing
   gut it, silt altering the
distribution of weight, the nature of content:
         whirlwinds move through it
or stand spinning like separate orders: the moon comes:
   there are barren spots: bogs, rising
by self-accretion from themselves, a growth into
         destruction of growth,
change of character,
   invasion of peat by poplar and oak: semi-precious
stones and precious metals drop from muddy water into mud:

it is an area of poise, really, held from tipping,
   dark wild water, fierce eels, countercurrents:
a habitat, precise ecology of forms
         mutually to some extent
tolerable, not entirely self-destroying: a crust afloat:

a scum, foam to the deep and other-natured:
but deeper than depth, too: a vacancy and swirl:

it may be spherical, light and knowledge merely
   the iris and opening
to the dark methods of its sight: how it comes and
       goes, ruptures and heals,
whirls and stands still: the moon comes: terrain.

Identity

1)   An individual spider web
     identifies a species:

an order of instinct prevails
     through all accidents of circumstance,
       though possibility is
high along the peripheries of
spider
           webs:
           you can go all
        around the fringing attachments

        and find
disorder ripe,
entropy rich, high levels of random,
     numerous occasions of accident:

2)   the possible settings
     of a web are infinite:

  how does
the spider keep
     identity
  while creating the web
  in a particular place?

  how and to what extent
     and by what modes of chemistry
     and control?

it is
wonderful

                how things work: I will tell you
                        about it
                        because

it is interesting
and because whatever is
moves in weeds
        and stars and spider webs
and known
                        is loved:
                in that love,
                each of us knowing it,
                I love you,

for it moves within and beyond us,
                sizzles in
winter grasses, darts and hangs with bumblebees
by summer windowsills:

                I will show you
the underlying that takes no image to itself,
                cannot be shown or said,
but weaves in and out of moons and bladderweeds,
                is all and
        beyond destruction
        because created fully in no
particular form:

                if the web were perfectly pre-set,
                the spider could
        never find
        a perfect place to set it in: and

                if the web were
perfectly adaptable,
if freedom and possibility were without limit,
                the web would
lose its special identity:

         the row-strung garden web
keeps order at the center
where space is freest (interesting that the freest
         "medium" should
         accept the firmest order)

and that
order
                  diminishes toward the
periphery
         allowing at the points of contact
                  entropy equal to entropy.

Jungle Knot

One morning Beebe
   found on a bank of the Amazon
an owl and snake
    dead in a coiled embrace:

   the vine prints its coil too deep into the tree
and leaved fire shoots greens of tender flame
    rising among the branches,
drawing behind a hardening, wooden clasp:

the tree does not
    generally escape
though it may live thralled for years,
  succumbing finally rather than at once,

    in the vine's victory
the casting of its eventual death,
   though it may live years
on the skeletal trunk,

termites rising, the rain softening,
  a limb in storm
falling, the vine air-free at last, structureless as death:
    the owl,

   Beebe says, underestimated
the anaconda's size: hunger had deformed
    sight or caution, or
anaconda, come out in moonlight on the river bank,

had left half his length in shade: (you
    sometimes tackle
more than just what the light shows):
  the owl struck talons

back of the anaconda's head
but weight grounded him in surprise: the anaconda
   coiled, embracing heaving wings
and cry, and the talons, squeezed in, sank

killing snake and owl in tightened pain:
   errors of vision, errors of self-defense!
errors of wisdom, errors of desire!
     the vulture dives, unlocks four eyes.

The Misfit

The unassimilable fact leads us on:
round the edges
    where broken shapes make poor masonry
the synthesis
fails (and succeeds) into limitation
    or extending itself too far

becomes a different synthesis:
law applies
    consistently to the molecule,
not to the ocean, unoriented, unprocessed,
it floats in, that floats in it:
    we are led on

to the boundaries
where relations loosen into chaos
    or where the nucleus fails to control,
fragments in odd shapes
expressing more and more the interstitial sea:
    we are led on

to peripheries, to the raw blocks of material,
where mortar and trowel can convert
    diversity into enlarging unity:
not the million oriented facts
but the one or two facts,
    out of place,

recalcitrant, the one observed fact
that tears us into questioning:
    what has not
joined dies into order to redeem, with
loss of singleness extends the form,
    or, unassimilable, leads us on.

Visit

It is not far to my place:
you can come smallboat,
pausing under shade in the eddies
   or going ashore
         to rest, regard the leaves

   or talk with birds and
shore weeds: hire a full grown man not
late in years to oar you
   and choose a canoe-like thin ship:
         (a dumb man is better and no

   costlier; he will attract
the reflections and silences under leaves:)
travel light: a single book, some twine:
the river is muscled at rapids with trout
   and a birch limb

   will make a suitable spit: if you
leave in the forenoon, you will arrive
with plenty of light
   the afternoon of the third day: I will
         come down to the landing

   (tell your man to look for it,
the dumb have clear sight and are free of
visions) to greet you with some made
   wine and a special verse:
         or you can come by shore:

   choose the right: there the rocks
cascade less frequently, the grade more gradual:

treat yourself gently: the ascent thins both
    mind and blood and you must
        keep still a dense reserve

    of silence we can poise against
conversation: there is little news:
I found last month a root with shape and
    have heard a new sound among
        the insects: come.

Expressions of Sea Level

Peripherally the ocean
marks itself
   against the gauging land
it erodes and
builds:

it is hard to name
the changeless:
speech without words,
   silence renders it:
and mid-ocean,

sky sealed unbroken to sea,
   there is no way to know
the ocean's speech,
intervolved and markless,
breaking against

   no boulder-held fingerland:
broken, surf things are expressions:
the sea speaks far from its core,
far from its center relinquishes the
long-held roar:

of any mid-sea
speech, the yielding resistances
of wind and water, spray,
swells, whitecaps, moans,
   it is a dream the sea makes,

an inner problem, a self-deep
dark and private anguish

revealed in small,
by hints, to
keen watchers on the shore:

only with the staid land
is the level conversation really held:
only in the meeting of rock and
    sea is
hard relevance shattered into light:

upbeach the clam shell
    holds smooth dry sand,
remembrance of tide:
water can go at
least that high: in

    the night, if you stay
to watch, or
if you come tomorrow at the right time,
you can see the shell caught
again in wash, the

sand turbulence changed,
new sand left smooth: if
the shell washes loose,
flops over,
    buries its rim in flux,

it will not be silence for
a shell that spoke: the
    half-buried back will
tell how the ocean dreamed
breakers against the land:

into the salt marshes the water comes fast with rising tide:
an inch of rise spreads by yards
    through tidal creeks, round fingerways of land:
the marsh grasses stem-logged

combine wind and water motions,
    slow from dry trembling
to heavier motions of wind translated through
cushioned stems; tide-held slant of grasses
    bent into the wind:

    is there a point of rest where
    the tide turns: is there one
    infinitely tiny higher touch
on the legs of egrets, the
skin of back, bay-eddy reeds:
    is there an instant when fullness is,
    without loss, complete: is there a
    statement perfect in its speech:

how do you know the moon
is moving: see the dry
casting of the beach worm
    dissolve at the
delicate rising touch:

that is the
    expression of sea level.
the talk of giants,
of ocean, moon, sun, of everything,
spoken in a dampened grain of sand.

One:Many

To maintain balance
between one and many by
    keeping in operation both one and many:

    fear a too great consistency, an arbitrary
imposition
    from the abstract *one*
    downwardly into the realities of manyness:
  this makes unity
not deriving from the balance of manyness
but by destruction of diversity:
  it is unity
      unavailable to change,
cut off from the reordering possibilities of
    variety:

      when I tried to summarize
      a moment's events
along the creek shore this afternoon,
the tide gathering momentum outwardly,
terns
hovering
dropping to spear shallow water,
  the minnows
in a band
wavering between deep and shallow water,
the sand hissing
into new images,
      the grass at its sound and symmetry,
      scoring
      semicircles of wind
  into sand,

the tan beetle in a footprint dead,
flickering to
    gusts of wind,
            the bloodsucking flies
            at their song and savage whirl,
when I tried to think by what
millions of grains of events
    the tidal creek had altered course,
        when I considered alone
a record
of the waves on the running blue creek,
    I was released into a power beyond my easy failures,
released to think
how so much freedom
        can keep the broad look of serenity
        and nearly statable balance:

not unity by the winnowing out of difference,
not unity thin and substanceless as abstraction,
    uneventful as theory:

I think of California's towns and ranges,
    deserts and oil fields,
highways, forests, white boulders,
        valleys, shorelines,
        headlands of rock;
and of Maine's
        unpainted seahouses
        way out on the tips of fingerlands,
lobster traps and pots,
freshwater lakes; of Chicago,
    hung like an eggsac on the leaf of Lake
Michigan, with
its
Art Museum, Prudential Building, Knickerbocker Hotel
(where Cummings stayed);
of North Carolina's
Pamlico and Albemarle Sounds, outer banks, shoals,
        telephone wire loads of swallows,

of Columbus County
              where fresh-dug peanuts
              are boiled
              in iron pots, salt filtering
in through boiled-clean shells (a delicacy
true
as artichokes or Jersey
asparagus): and on and on through the villages,
along dirt roads, ditchbanks, by gravel pits and on
   to the homes, to the citizens and their histories,
inventions, longings:
I think how enriching, though unassimilable as a whole
into art, are the differences: the small-business
man in
       Kansas City declares an extra dividend
and his daughter
              who teaches school in Duquesne
buys a Volkswagen, a second car for the family:
out of many, one:
from variety an over-riding unity, the expression of
variety:

no book of laws, short of unattainable reality itself,
can anticipate every event,
control every event: only the book of laws founded
     against itself,
founded on freedom of each event to occur as itself,
lasts into the inevitable balances events will take.

Still

I said I will find what is lowly
    and put the roots of my identity
    down there:
each day I'll wake up
and find the lowly nearby,
    a handy focus and reminder,
a ready measure of my significance,
the voice by which I would be heard,
the wills, the kinds of selfishness
    I could
freely adopt as my own:

but though I have looked everywhere,
    I can find nothing
    to give myself to:
    everything is

magnificent with existence, is in
surfeit of glory:
nothing is diminished,
nothing has been diminished for me:

I said what is more lowly than the grass:
    ah, underneath,
    a ground-crust of dry-burnt moss:
    I looked at it closely
and said this can be my habitat: but
nestling in I
found
    below the brown exterior
    green mechanisms beyond intellect
awaiting resurrection in rain: so I got up

and ran saying there is nothing lowly in the universe:
I found a beggar:
he had stumps for legs: nobody was paying
him any attention: everybody went on by:
    I nestled in and found his life:
there, love shook his body like a devastation:
I said
    though I have looked everywhere
    I can find nothing lowly
    in the universe:

I whirled through transfigurations up and down,
transfigurations of size and shape and place:
    at one sudden point came still,
    stood in wonder:
moss, beggar, weed, tick, pine, self, magnificent
    with being!

Corsons Inlet

I went for a walk over the dunes again this morning
to the sea,
then turned right along
   the surf
                  rounded a naked headland
                  and returned

   along the inlet shore:

it was muggy sunny, the wind from the sea steady and high,
crisp in the running sand,
      some breakthroughs of sun
   but after a bit

continuous overcast:

the walk liberating, I was released from forms,
from the perpendiculars,
      straight lines, blocks, boxes, binds
of thought
into the hues, shadings, rises, flowing bends and blends
            of sight:

                  I allow myself eddies of meaning:
yield to a direction of significance
running
like a stream through the geography of my work:
   you can find
in my sayings
                  swerves of action
                  like the inlet's cutting edge:
            there are dunes of motion,
organizations of grass, white sandy paths of remembrance
in the overall wandering of mirroring mind:

but Overall is beyond me: is the sum of these events
I cannot draw, the ledger I cannot keep, the accounting
beyond the account:

in nature there are few sharp lines: there are areas of
primrose
         more or less dispersed;
disorderly orders of bayberry; between the rows
of dunes,
irregular swamps of reeds,
though not reeds alone, but grass, bayberry, yarrow, all . . .
predominantly reeds:

I have reached no conclusions, have erected no boundaries,
shutting out and shutting in, separating inside
         from outside: I have
         drawn no lines:
         as

manifold events of sand
change the dune's shape that will not be the same shape
tomorrow,

so I am willing to go along, to accept
the becoming
thought, to stake off no beginnings or ends, establish
         no walls:

by transitions the land falls from grassy dunes to creek
to undercreek: but there are no lines, though
         change in that transition is clear
         as any sharpness: but "sharpness" spread out,
allowed to occur over a wider range
than mental lines can keep:

the moon was full last night: today, low tide was low:
black shoals of mussels exposed to the risk
of air
and, earlier, of sun,

waved in and out with the waterline, waterline inexact,
caught always in the event of change:
>   a young mottled gull stood free on the shoals
>   and ate
to vomiting: another gull, squawking possession, cracked a crab,
picked out the entrails, swallowed the soft-shelled legs, a ruddy
turnstone running in to snatch leftover bits:

risk is full: every living thing in
siege: the demand is life, to keep life: the small
white blacklegged egret, how beautiful, quietly stalks and spears
>   the shallows, darts to shore
>   to stab—what? I couldn't
>   see against the black mudflats—a frightened
>   fiddler crab?

>   the news to my left over the dunes and
reeds and bayberry clumps was
>   fall: thousands of tree swallows
>   gathering for flight:
>   an order held
>   in constant change: a congregation
rich with entropy: nevertheless, separable, noticeable
>   as one event,
>   not chaos: preparations for
flight from winter,
cheet, cheet, cheet, cheet, wings rifling the green clumps,
beaks
at the bayberries
>   a perception full of wind, flight, curve,
>   sound:
>   the possibility of rule as the sum of rulelessness:
the "field" of action
with moving, incalculable center:

in the smaller view, order tight with shape:
blue tiny flowers on a leafless weed: carapace of crab:
snail shell:
>   pulsations of order

45

in the bellies of minnows: orders swallowed,
broken down, transferred through membranes
to strengthen larger orders: but in the large view, no
lines or changeless shapes: the working in and out, together
and against, of millions of events: this,
so that I make
no form of
formlessness:

orders as summaries, as outcomes of actions override
or in some way result, not predictably (seeing me gain
the top of a dune,
the swallows
could take flight—some other fields of bayberry
could enter fall
berryless) and there is serenity:

no arranged terror: no forcing of image, plan,
or thought:
no propaganda, no humbling of reality to precept:

terror pervades but is not arranged, all possibilities
of escape open: no route shut, except in
the sudden loss of all routes:

I see narrow orders, limited tightness, but will
not run to that easy victory:
still around the looser, wider forces work:
I will try
to fasten into order enlarging grasps of disorder, widening
scope, but enjoying the freedom that
Scope eludes my grasp, that there is no finality of vision,
that I have perceived nothing completely,
that tomorrow a new walk is a new walk.

Saliences

Consistencies rise
and ride
the mind down
hard routes
    walled
with no outlet and so
to open a variable geography,
    proliferate
possibility, here
is this dune fest
    releasing
mind feeding out,
gathering clusters,
fields of order in disorder,
where choice
can make beginnings,
    turns,
    reversals,
where straight line
and air-hard thought
can meet
unarranged disorder,
    dissolve
before the one event that
creates present time
in the multi-variable
    scope:
a variable of wind
among the dunes,
making variables
of position and direction and sound
of every reed leaf

and bloom,
running streams of sand,
winding, rising, at a depression
falling out into deltas,
weathering shells with blast,
striking hiss into clumps of grass,
against bayberry leaves,
   lifting
the spider from footing to footing
hard across the dry even crust
toward the surf:
wind, a variable, soft wind, hard
steady wind, wind
shaped and kept in the
bent of trees,
the prevailing dipping seaward
of reeds,
the kept and erased sandcrab trails:
wind, the variable to the gull's flight,
how and where he drops the clam
and the way he heads in, running to loft:
wind, from the sea, high surf
and cool weather;
from the land, a lessened breakage
and the land's heat:
wind alone as a variable,
as a factor in millions of events,
leaves no two moments
on the dunes the same:
   keep
free to these events,
bend to these
changing weathers:
multiple as sand, events of sense
alter old dunes
of mind,
release new channels of flow,
free materials
to new forms:

wind alone as a variable
takes this neck of dunes
out of calculation's reach:
come out of the hard
routes and ruts,
pour over the walls
of previous assessments: turn to
the open,
the unexpected, to new saliences of feature.

*

The reassurance is
that through change
continuities sinuously work,
cause and effect
    without alarm,
gradual shadings out or in,
motions that full
    with time
do not surprise, no
abrupt leap or burst: possibility,
with meaningful development
of circumstance:

when I went back to the dunes today,
    saliences,
congruent to memory,
spread firmingly across my sight:
the narrow white path
rose and dropped over
grassy rises toward the sea:
sheets of reeds,
tasseling now near fall,
filled the hollows
with shapes of ponds or lakes:
bayberry, darker, made wandering
chains of clumps, sometimes pouring
into heads, like stopped water:
    much seemed

constant, to be looked
forward to, expected:
from the top of a dune rise,
look of ocean salience: in
   the hollow,
where a runlet
   makes in
at full tide and fills a bowl,
extravagance of pink periwinkle
along the grassy edge,
and a blue, bunchy weed, deep blue,
deep into the mind the dark blue
   constant:
minnows left high in the tide-deserted pocket,
   fiddler crabs
bringing up gray pellets of drying sand,
disappearing from air's faster events
at any close approach:
certain things and habits
   recognizable as
having lasted through the night:
though what change in
a day's doing!
desertions of swallows
   that yesterday
ravaged air, bush, reed, attention
in gatherings wide as this neck of dunes:
now, not a sound
or shadow, no trace of memory, no remnant
   explanation:
summations of permanence!
where not a single single thing endures,
the overall reassures,
deaths and flights,
shifts and sudden assaults claiming
limited orders,
the separate particles:
earth brings to grief
much in an hour that sang, leaped, swirled,
yet keeps a round
   quiet turning,
beyond loss or gain,
beyond concern for the separate reach.

Dunes

Taking root in windy sand
    is not an easy
way
to go about
    finding a place to stay.

A ditchbank or wood's-edge
    has firmer ground.

In a loose world though
    something can be started—
a root touch water,
    a tip break sand—

Mounds from that can rise
    on held mounds,
a gesture of building, keeping,
    a trapping
into shape.

Firm ground is not available ground.

Center

A bird fills up the
streamside bush
with wasteful song,
capsizes waterfall,
mill run, and
superhighway
to
song's improvident
center
lost in the green
bush green
answering bush:
wind varies:
the noon sun casts
mesh refractions
on the stream's amber
bottom
and nothing at all gets,
nothing gets
caught at all.

Reflective

I found a
weed
that had a

mirror in it
and that
mirror

looked in at
a mirror
in

me that
had a
weed in it

Winter Scene

There is now not a single
leaf on the cherry tree:

except when the jay
plummets in, lights, and,

in pure clarity, squalls:
then every branch

quivers and
breaks out in blue leaves.

Mountain Talk

I was going along a dusty highroad
when the mountain
across the way
turned me to its silence:
oh I said how come
I don't know your
massive symmetry and rest:
nevertheless, said the mountain,
would you want
to be
lodged here with
a changeless prospect, risen
to an unalterable view:
so I went on
counting my numberless fingers.

Loss

When the sun
falls behind the sumac
thicket the
wild
yellow daisies
in diffuse evening shade
lose their
rigorous attention
and
half-wild with loss
turn
any way the wind does
and lift their
petals up
to float
off their stems
and go

Recovery

All afternoon
the tree shadows, accelerating,
lengthened
till
sunset
shot them black into infinity:
next morning
darkness
returned from the other
infinity and the
shadows caught ground
and through the morning, slowing,
hardened into noon.

Laser

An image comes
and the mind's light, confused
as that on surf
or ocean shelves,
gathers up,
parallelizes, focuses
and in a rigid beam illuminates the image:

the head seeks in itself
fragments of left-over light
to cast a new
direction,
any direction,
to strike and fix
a random, contradicting image:

but any found image falls
back to darkness or
the lesser beams splinter and
go out:
the mind tries to
dream of diversity, of mountain
rapids shattered with sound and light,

of wind fracturing brush or
bursting out of order against a mountain
range: but the focused beam
folds all energy in:
the image glares filling all space:
the head falls and
hangs and cannot wake itself.

Height

There was a hill once wanted
to become a mountain
     and
forces underground helped it
  lift itself
  into broad view
and noticeable height:

but the green hills around and even
some passable mountains,
    diminished by white,
wanted it down
so the mountain, alone, found
  grandeur taxing and
  turned and turned
to try to be concealed:

oh but after the rock is
massive and high . . !
    how many centuries of rain and
ice, avalanche
and shedding shale
  before the dull mound
can yield to grass!

He Held Radical Light

He held radical light
as music in his skull: music
turned, as
over ridges immanences of evening light
rise, turned
back over the furrows of his brain
into the dark, shuddered,
shot out again
in long swaying swirls of sound:

reality had little weight in his transcendence
so he
had trouble keeping
his feet on the ground, was
terrified by that
and liked himself, and others, mostly
under roofs:
nevertheless, when the
light churned and changed

his head to music, nothing could keep him
off the mountains, his
head back, mouth working,
wrestling to say, to cut loose
from the high, unimaginable hook:
released, hidden from stars, he ate,
burped, said he was like any one
of us: demanded he
was like any one of us.

Poetics

I look for the way
things will turn
out spiralling from a center,
the shape
things will take to come forth in

so that the birch tree white
touched black at branches
will stand out
wind-glittering
totally its apparent self:

I look for the forms
things want to come as

from what black wells of possibility,
how a thing will
unfold:

not the shape on paper—though
that, too—but the
uninterfering means on paper:

not so much looking for the shape
as being available
to any shape that may be
summoning itself
through me
from the self not mine but ours.

Cascadilla Falls

I went down by Cascadilla
Falls this
evening, the
stream below the falls,
and picked up a
handsized stone
kidney-shaped, testicular, and

thought all its motions into it,
the 800 mph earth spin,
the 190-million-mile yearly
displacement around the sun,
the overriding
grand
haul

of the galaxy with the 30,000
mph of where
the sun's going:
thought all the interweaving
motions
into myself: dropped

the stone to dead rest:
the stream from other motions
broke
rushing over it:
shelterless,
I turned

to the sky and stood still:
oh
I do
not know where I am going
that I can live my life
by this single creek.

Love Song

Like the hills under dusk you
fall away from the light:
you deepen: the green
light darkens
and you are nearly lost:
only so much light as
stars keep
manifests your face:
the total night in
myself raves
for the light along your lips.

Love Song (2)

Rings of birch bark
stand in the woods
still circling the nearly
vanished log: after
we go to pass
through log and star
this white song will
hug us together in the
woods of some lover's head.

Involved

They say last night radiation
storms spilled down the meridians,
cool green tongues of solar
flares, non-human & not
to be humanized, licking at
human life: an arctic
air mass shielded us: had I been
out I'd have said,
knowing them masked, burn me: or
thanks for the show:
my spine would have flared
sympathetic colors:
as it is I slept through,
burning from a distant source.

Project

My subject's
still the wind still
difficult to
present
being invisible:
nevertheless should I
presume it not
I'd be compelled
to say
how the honeysuckle bushlimbs
wave themselves:
difficult
beyond presumption

Offset

Losing information he
rose gaining
view
till at total
loss gain was
extreme:
extreme & invisible:
the eye
seeing nothing
lost its
separation:
self-song
(that is a mere motion)
fanned out
into failing swirls
slowed &
became continuum.

The Quince Bush

The flowering quince bush
on the back hedge has been
run through by a morning
glory vine

and this morning three blooms
are open as if for all light,
sound, and motion: their adjustment
to light is

pink, though they reach for
stellar reds and core violets:
they listen as if for racket's
inner silence

and focus, as if to starve, all motion:
patterns of escaped sea
they tip the defeated, hostile,
oceanic wind:

elsewhere young men scratch and fire:
a troubled child shudders to a freeze:
an old man bursts finally and
rattles down

clacking slats: the caterpillar pierced
by a wasp egg blooms inside with
the tender worm: wailing
walls float

luminous with the charge of grief:
a day pours through a morning glory
dayblossom's adequate, poised,
available center.

Small Song

The reeds give
way to the

wind and give
the wind away

Script

The blackbird takes out
from the thicket down there
uphill toward
the house, shoots
through a vacancy in the
elm tree & bolts
over the house:
some circling leaves waving
record
size, direction, and speed.

Square

The formulation that
saves damns:
consequently (unsavable)
a periphery riffler
I thread the
outskirts of mandate,
near enough
to be knowingly away &
far enough away to
wind and snap through
riddling underbrush.

Correction

The burdens of the world
on my back
lighten the world
not a whit while
removing them greatly
decreases my specific
gravity

Help

From the inlet
surf a father
pulls in a crab—
a wonderful machinery
but
not a fish: kicks
it off the line &
up the beach
where three daughters
and two sons take
turns bringing cups
of water
to keep alive, to
watch work, the sanded
& disjeweled.

Photosynthesis

The sun's wind
blows the fire
green, sails the
chloroplasts,
lifts banks, bogs,
boughs into flame:
the green ash of
yellow loss.

The Account

The difference, finding the
difference: earth, no heavier
with me here, will be no
lighter when I'm gone: sum or
subtraction equals zero: no
change—not to the loss of a
single electron's spin—will
net from my total change:
is that horror or opportunity:
should I spurn earth now with
mind, toss my own indifference
to indifference, invent some
other scale that assents to
temporary weight, make something
substanceless as love earth can't
get to with changeless changing:
will my electrical system noumenally
at the last moment leap free
and, weightless, will it
have any way to deal—or if
there is some thinnest weight,
what will it join with, how
will it neighbor: something finer
than perception, a difference
so opposite to ground it will
have no mass, indifferent to mass.

Holly

The hollybush flowers
small whites (become of
course berries)
four tiny petals
turned
back and four
anthers stuck out:
the pistil low &
honey-high:
wasp-bees (those small
wasps or
bees) come around
with a glee too
fine to hear: when
the wind dies
at dusk, silence,
unaffronted,
puts a robe
slightly thinner
than sight over
all the flowers
so darkness &
the terrible stars
will not hurt them.

The Confirmers

The saints are gathering at the real
places, trying tough skin on sharp
   conscience,
endurance in the hot spots—
searching out to define, come up
against, mouth
the bitterest bit:
you can hear them yelping
down in the dark greeny groves of
   condemnation:
their lips slice back
with jittery suctions, cold
insweeps of conjured grief:
if they, footloose, wham up the
precise damnation,
   consolation
may be no more than us trudging
down from paunchy dinners,
swatting hallelujah arms at
dusk bugs and telling them pure
terror has obviously made them
earnest of mind and of motion lithe.

Snow Log

Especially the fallen tree
the snow picks
out in the woods to show:

the snow means nothing by that,
no special emphasis: actually
snow picks nothing out:

but was it a failure, is it,
snow's responsible for
that the brittle upright black

shrubs and small trees
set off what caught the snow
in special light:

or there's some intention
behind the snow snow's too shallow
to reckon with: I take it on myself:

especially the fallen tree
the snow picks
out in the woods to show.

Classic

I sat by a stream in a
perfect—except for willows—
emptiness
and the mountain that
was around,

scraggly with brush &
rock
said
I see you're scribbling again:

accustomed to mountains,
their cumbersome intrusions,
I said

well, yes, but in a fashion very
like the water here
uncapturable and vanishing:

but that
said the mountain does not
excuse the stance
or diction

and next if you're not careful
you'll be
arriving at ways
water survives its motions.

Clarity

After the event the rockslide
realized,
in a still diversity of completion,
grain and fissure,
declivity
&
force of upheaval,
whether rain slippage,
ice crawl, root
explosion or
stream erosive undercut:

well I said it is a pity:
one swath of sight will never
be the same: nonetheless,
this
shambles has
relieved a bind, a taut of twist,
revealing streaks &
scores of knowledge
now obvious and quiet.

Periphery

One day I complained about the periphery
that it was thickets hard to get around in
    or get around for
an older man: it's like keeping charts

of symptoms, every reality a symptom
where the ailment's not nailed down:
    much knowledge, precise enough,
but so multiple it says this man is alive

or isn't: it's like all of a body answering
all of pharmacopoeia, a too
    adequate relationship:
so I complained and said maybe I'd brush

deeper and see what was pushing all this
periphery, so difficult to make any sense
    out of, out:
with me, decision brings its own

hesitation: a symptom, no doubt, but open
and meaningless enough without paradigm:
    but hesitation
can be all right, too: I came on a spruce

thicket full of elk, gushy snow-weed,
nine species of lichen, four pure white
    rocks and
several swatches of verbena near bloom.

Upland

Certain presuppositions are altered
by height: the inversion to
sky-well a peak
in a desert makes: the welling

from clouds down the boulder fountains:
it is always a
surprise out west there—
the blue ranges loose and aglide

with heat and then come close
on slopes leaning up into green:
a number of other phenomena might
be summoned—

take the Alleghenies for example,
some quality in the air
of summit stones lying free and loose
out among the shrub trees: every

exigency seems prepared for that might
roll, bound, or give flight
to stone: that is, the stones are
prepared: they are round and ready.

Cut the Grass

The wonderful workings of the world: wonderful,
wonderful: I'm surprised half the time:
ground up fine, I puff if a pebble stirs:

I'm nervous: my morality's intricate: if
a squash blossom dies, I feel withered as a stained
zucchini and blame my nature: and

when grassblades flop to the little red-ant
queens burring around trying to get aloft, I blame
my not keeping the grass short, stubble

firm: well, I learn a lot of useless stuff, meant
to be ignored: like when the sun sinking in the
west glares a plane invisible, I think how much

revelation concealment necessitates: and then I
think of the ocean, multiple to a blinding
oneness and realize that only total expression

expresses hiding: I'll have to say everything
to take on the roundness and withdrawal of the deep dark:
less than total is a bucketful of radiant toys.

Further On

Up this high and far north
it's shale and woodsless snow:
small willows and alder brush

mark out melt streams on the
opposite slope and the wind talks
as much as it can before freeze

takes the gleeful, glimmering
tongues away: whips and sticks
will scream and screech then

all winter over the deaf heights,
the wind lifting its saying out
to the essential yell of the

lost and gone: it's summer now:
elk graze the high meadows:
marshgrass heads high as a moose's

ears: lichen, a wintery weed,
fills out for the brittle sleep:
waterbirds plunder the shallows.

If Anything Will Level with You Water Will

Streams shed out of mountains in a white rust
(such the abomination of height)
slow then into upland basins or high marsh

and slowing drop loose composed figurations
on big river bottoms
or give the first upward turn from plains:

that's for modern streams: if sediment's
lithified it
may have to be considered ancient, the result of

a pressing, perhaps lengthy, induration:
old streams from which the water's
vanished are interesting, I mean that

kind of tale,
water, like spirit, jostling hard stuff around
to make speech into one of its realest expressions:

water certainly is interesting (as is spirit) and
small rock, a glacial silt, just as much so:
but most pleasurable (magma & migma) is

rock itself in a bound slurp or spill
or overthrust into very recent times:
there waterlike stone, those heated seekings &

goings, cools to exact concentration, I
mean the telling's unmediated:
the present allows the reading of much

old material: but none of it need be read:
it says itself (and
said itself) so to speak perfectly in itself.

Conserving the Magnitude of Uselessness

Spits of glitter in lowgrade ore,
precious stones too poorly surrounded for harvest,
to all things not worth the work
of having,

brush oak on a sharp slope, for example,
the balk tonnage of woods-lodged boulders,
the irreparable desert,
drowned river mouths, lost shores where

the winged and light-footed go,
take creosote bush that possesses
ground nothing else will have,
to all things and for all things

crusty or billowy with indifference,
for example, incalculable, irremovable water
or fluvio-glacial deposits
larch or dwarf aspen in the least breeze sometimes shiver in—

suddenly the salvation of waste betides,
the peerlessly unsettled seas that shape the continents,
take the gales wasting and in waste over
Antarctica and the sundry high shoals of ice,

for the inexcusable (the worthless abundant) the
merely tiresome, the obviously unimprovable,
to these and for these and for their undiminishment
the poets will yelp and hoot forever

probably,
rank as weeds themselves and just as abandoned:
nothing useful is of lasting value:
dry wind only is still talking among the oldest stones.

Plunder

I have appropriated the windy twittering of aspen leaves
into language, stealing something from reality like a
silverness: drop-scapes of ice from peak sheers:

much of the rise in brooks over slow-rolled glacial stones:
the loop of reeds over the shallow's edge when birds
feed on the rafts of algae: I have taken right out of the

air the clear streaks of bird music and held them in my
head like shifts of sculpture glint: I have sent language
through the mud roils of a raccoon's paws like a net,

netting the roils: made my own uses of a downwind's
urgency on a downward stream: held with a large scape
of numbness the black distance upstream to the mountains

flashing and bursting: meanwhile, everything else, frog,
fish, bear, gnat has turned in its provinces and made off
with its uses: my mind's indicted by all I've taken.

Triphammer Bridge

I wonder what to mean by *sanctuary*, if a real or
apprehended place, as of a bell rung in a gold
surround, or as of silver roads along the beaches

of clouds seas don't break or black mountains
overspill; jail: ice here's shapelier than anything,
on the eaves massive, jawed along gorge ledges, solid

in the plastic blue boat fall left water in: if I
think the bitterest thing I can think of that seems like
reality, slickened back, hard, shocked by rip-high wind:

sanctuary, *sanctuary*, I say it over and over and the
word's sound is the one place to dwell: that's it, just
the sound, and the imagination of the sound—a place.

The City Limits

When you consider the radiance, that it does not withhold
itself but pours its abundance without selection into every
nook and cranny not overhung or hidden; when you consider

that birds' bones make no awful noise against the light but
lie low in the light as in a high testimony; when you consider
the radiance, that it will look into the guiltiest

swervings of the weaving heart and bear itself upon them,
not flinching into disguise or darkening; when you consider
the abundance of such resource as illuminates the glow-blue

bodies and gold-skeined wings of flies swarming the dumped
guts of a natural slaughter or the coil of shit and in no
way winces from its storms of generosity; when you consider

that air or vacuum, snow or shale, squid or wolf, rose or lichen,
each is accepted into as much light as it will take, then
the heart moves roomier, the man stands and looks about, the

leaf does not increase itself above the grass, and the dark
work of the deepest cells is of a tune with May bushes
and fear lit by the breadth of such calmly turns to praise.

Right On

The tamarack can cut rain down to size, mist-little
bead-gauze, hold at needlepoint a plenty
and from the going, blue-sunk storm keep a

shadow, glittery recollection: the heart-leaved
big hydrangea bends over blossom-nodding, a few
large drops and a general glaze streaking leaves

with surface tension: the maple leaves
gather hail-size drops at the lobes and
sway them ragged loose: spirea, quince, cedar,

elm, hollyhock, clover (a sharp beader)
permit various styles of memory: then the sun
breaks out and clears the record of what is gone.

Rectitude

Last night's thunderstorm's
glancing quick shifts of strong wind and
heavy sheets of tensed up
beating down rain

have left the snapdragons
velvet-hung in red bead
bedraggled, a
disorientation extreme:

but this morning,
the clouds clearing, the sun
breaking its one source out,
light is working in the stems' cells,

drawing up, adjusting, soft alignments
coming true, and pretty soon
now the prevailing command "attention!"
will seem to have been uttered suddenly.

Sorting

There's not much hill left up from here and after
rains runlets lose head quickly to the least
quiver: height has such poverty of

reservoir, and in a drought poplars will go
brittle with yearning and take lightly their usual
mass and rock-hold, while at the bottom of the

ridge, the fountains will still be blinking,
the glade weeds rushed green: well, at least, we get
some view up here and sometimes breezes that miss

the valley cut a high sweep across from ridge to ridge
and then most often the drought will break
in time, the trees come back, a branch or two burnished.

Viable

Motion's the dead give away,
eye catcher, the revealing risk:
the caterpillar sulls on the hot macadam

but then, risking, ripples to the bush:
the cricket, startled, leaps the
quickest arc: the earthworm, casting,

nudges a grassblade, and the sharp robin
strikes: sound's the other
announcement: the redbird lands in

an elm branch and tests the air with
cheeps for an answering, reassuring
cheep, for a motion already cleared:

survival organizes these means down to
tension, to enwrapped, twisting suasions:
every act or non-act enceinte with risk or

prize: why must the revelations be
sound and motion, the poet, too, moving and
saying through the scary opposites to death.

Delaware Water Gap

Rounding the mountain's rim-ledge,
we looked out valleyward
onto the summits of lesser hills,

summits bottoms of held air, still lesser
heights clefts and ravines: oh, I said,
the land's a slow ocean, the long blue

ridge a reared breakage, these small peaks
dips and rises: we're floating,
I said, intermediates of stone and air,

and nothing has slowed altogether
into determination and a new wave
to finish this one is building up somewhere,

a continent crowded loose, upwarping
against its suasions, we, you and I,
to be drowned, now so sustained and free.

Day

On a cold late
September morning,
wider than sky-wide
discs of lit-shale clouds

skim the hills,
crescents, chords
of sunlight
now and then fracturing

the long peripheries:
the crow flies
silent,
on course but destinationless,

floating:
hurry, hurry,
the running light says,
while anything remains.

Staking Claim

Look, look where the mind can go
I said to the sanctified
willows
wreathing jittery slow slopes of wind

look it can go up up to the ultimate
node where
remembering is foretelling
generation, closure
where taking in is giving out
ascent and descent a common blip

look going like wind over rocks
it can
touch where
completion is cancellation

all the way to the final vacant core
that brings
things together and turns them away

all the way away
to stirless bliss!

and the willows,
dream-wraiths song-turned,
bent in troops of unanimity,
never could waken
never could feel the rushing days

never could feel the cold
wind and rushing days
or thoroughly know
their leaves taking flight:

look I said to the willows
what the mind
can apprehend,

entire and perfect staying,
and yet face winter's
face coming over the hill

look I said to the leaves
breaking into flocks around me taking
my voice away
to the far side of the hill
and way beyond gusting down the long changes

The Eternal City

After the explosion or cataclysm, that big
display that does its work but then fails
out with destructions, one is left with the

pieces: at first, they don't look very valuable,
but nothing sizable remnant around for
gathering the senses on, one begins to take

an interest, to sort out, to consider closely
what will do and won't, matters having become
not only small but critical: bulbs may have been

uprooted: they should be eaten, if edible, or
got back in the ground: what used to be garages,
even the splinters, should be collected for

fires: some unusually deep holes or cleared
woods may be turned to water supplies or
sudden fields: ruinage is hardly ever a

pretty sight but it must when splendor goes
accept into itself piece by piece all the old
perfect human visions, all the old perfect loves.

Phase

These still days after frost have let down
the maple leaves in a straight compression
to the grass, a slight wobble from circular to

the east, as if sometime, probably at night, the
wind's moved that way—surely, nothing else
could have done it, really eliminating the *as*

if, although the *as if* can nearly stay since
the wind may have been a big, slow
one, imperceptible, but still angling

off the perpendicular the leaves' fall:
anyway, there was the green-ribbed, yellow,
flat-open reduction: I just now bagged it up.

Eyesight

It was May before my
attention came
to spring and

my word I said
to the southern slopes
I've

missed it, it
came and went before
I got right to see:

don't worry, said the mountain,
try the later northern slopes
or if

you can climb, climb
into spring: but
said the mountain

it's not that way
with all things, some
that go are gone

The Arc Inside and Out

for Harold Bloom

If, whittler and dumper, gross carver
into the shadiest curvings, I took branch
and meat from the stalk of life, threw

away the monies of the treasured,
treasurable mind, cleaved memory free
of the instant, if I got right down

shucking off periphery after periphery
to the glassy vague gray parabolas
and swoops of unnailable perception,

would I begin to improve the purity,
would I essentialize out the distilled
form, the glitter-stone that whether

the world comes or goes clicks gleams
and chinks of truth self-making, never
to be shuttered, the face-brilliant core

stone: or if I, amasser, heap shoveler,
depth pumper, took in all springs and
oceans, paramoecia and moons, massive

buttes and summit slants, rooted trunks
and leafages, anthologies of wise words,
schemata, all grasses (including the

tidal *Spartinas*, marginal, salty
broadsweeps) would I finally come on a
suasion, large, fully-informed, restful

scape, turning back in on itself, its
periphery enclosing our system with
its bright dot and allowing in nonparlant

quantities at the edge void, void, and
void, would I then feel plenitude
brought to center and extent, a sweet

easing away of all edge, evil, and surprise:
these two ways to dream! dreaming them's
the bumfuzzlement—the impoverished

diamond, the heterogeneous abundance
starved into oneness: ultimately, either
way, which is our peace, the little

arc-line appears, inside which is nothing,
outside which is nothing—however big,
nothing beyond: however small, nothing

within: neither way to go's to stay, stay
here, the apple an apple with its own hue
or streak, the drink of water, the drink,

the falling into sleep, restfully ever the
falling into sleep, dream, dream, and
every morning the sun comes, the sun.

Uppermost

The top
grain on the peak
weighs next
to nothing and,
sustained
by a mountain,
has no burden,
but nearly
ready to float,
exposed
to summit wind,
it endures
the rigors of having
no further
figure to complete
and a
blank sky
to guide its dreaming

Bonus

The hemlocks slumped
already as if bewailing
the branch-loading

shales of ice, the rain
changes and a snow
sifty as fog

begins to fall, brightening
the ice's bruise-glimmer
with white holdings:

the hemlocks, muffled,
deepen to the grim
taking of a further beauty on.

For Harold Bloom

I went to the summit and stood in the high nakedness:
the wind tore about this
way and that in confusion and its speech could not
get through to me nor could I address it:
still I said as if to the alien in myself
    I do not speak to the wind now:
for having been brought this far by nature I have been
brought out of nature
and nothing here shows me the image of myself:
for the word *tree* I have been shown a tree
and for the word *rock* I have been shown a rock,
for stream, for cloud, for star
this place has provided firm implication and answering
    but where here is the image for *longing:*
so I touched the rocks, their interesting crusts:
I flaked the bark of stunt-fir:
I looked into space and into the sun
and nothing answered my word *longing:*
    goodbye, I said, goodbye, nature so grand and
reticent, your tongues are healed up into their own
element
and as you have shut up you have shut me out: I am
as foreign here as if I had landed, a visitor:
so I went back down and gathered mud
and with my hands made an image for *longing:*
    I took the image to the summit: first
I set it here, on the top rock, but it completed
nothing: then I set it there among the tiny firs
but it would not fit:
so I returned to the city and built a house to set
the image in
and men came into my house and said
    that is an image for *longing*
and nothing will ever be the same again

Index of Titles and First Lines